salmonpoetry

Diverse Voices from Ireland and the World

In Praise of Urban Living

JOSEPH HORGAN

Published in 2024 by
Salmon Poetry
Cliffs of Moher, County Clare, Ireland
Website: www.salmonpoetry.com
Email: info@salmonpoetry.com

Copyright © Joseph Horgan, 2024

ISBN 978-1-915022-44-8

All rights reserved. No part of this publication may be reproduced or transmitted in any form or by any means, electronic or mechanical, including photography, recording, or any information storage or retrieval system, without permission in writing from the publisher. The book is sold subject to the condition that it shall not, by way of trade or otherwise, be lent, resold or otherwise circulated without the publisher's prior consent in any form of binding or cover other than that in which it is published and without a similar condition, including this condition, being imposed on the subsequent purchaser.

Cover Image by Rachel Libeskind from a theatre piece by Tadeusz Kantor
Cover Design & Typesetting by Siobhán Hutson Jeanotte

Printed in Ireland by Sprint Print

Salmon Poetry gratefully acknowledges the support of
The Arts Council / An Chomhairle Ealaíon

for Antony Owen, poet

Acknowledgements

With thanks to the editors who have published or broadcast a number of these poems in the following places:

BELLEVILLE PARK PAGES
BRAND
BURNING BUSH2
HEADSTUFF
I AM NOT A SILENT POET
IRISH LEFT REVIEW
L'ALLURE DES MOTS
PARIS LIT UP
POETRY IRELAND REVIEW
POETRY SALZBURG REVIEW
PROLETARIAN POETRY
RTE THE POETRY PROGRAMME
THE BOGMAN'S CANNON
THE CHIRON REVIEW
THE STINGING FLY
THE STONY THURSDAY BOOK

A section of this collection was completed during a residency at the Heinrich Böll Cottage on Achill Island for which the author wishes to give thanks.

Contents

I LOVE A MAN	11
THE BEST DAY EVER, ASRAEL	12
THE GLISTENING SUN ON THE GLISTENING STREET	13
CONCEALMENT	15
LIFE ON PUBLIC TRANSPORT	16
CHANGE OF ADDRESS	17
WORKING NIGHTS WHILE THE POETS READ	18
THE MAPS YOU TOOK WITH YOU WHEN YOU WENT	19
IMPERIAL ROAD	20
UNLAWFUL OATHS	21
WE WENT TO SCHOOL IN A BALLOON	22
AFTER THE BATTLE OF SALTLEY GATES	23
LOVE SONG	24
THE CITY IS FUNDAMENTAL	25
LATE NIGHT NOTES OF THE EMIGRANT	26
THE ECONOMIC SYSTEM IN A TIME OF SURPLUS	27
A WHOLE SENSIBILITY	28
THE SOUND OF PUBLIC SPACES	29
LOST AFTERNOONS	30
GREEN FIRST SPACES FORM THE CORE OF URBAN LIVING	31
LIKE CLOCKWORK	32
ALL YOUR RELATIVES DISTANT AND CLOSE GATHER BY THE RIVER THAT RUNS THROUGH EACH CITY	33
THE COUNTY COUNCILLOR'S HOUSE	34
YOU BRING OUT THE CITY IN ME	35
BIRMINGHAM	37
MODES OF TRANSPORT AS A SPIRIT LEVEL SIGNIFIER OF CLASS STRUCTURE	38
THREE O'CLOCK FIXTURE LIST	39
WHAT HAPPENED AFTERWARDS	40
NIGHTSHIFT	41
THE REVOLUTIONARIES FIRST TAKE OVER THE STATE BROADCASTER	42

ALL THE ADDRESSES IN ALL OF THE CITIES	43
SONGS WE SING ABOUT OURSELVES	44
HIGHWIRE	45
THOUGH WHEN THEY CATCH MY EYE	46
WAITING TO BEGIN WHAT WORK IS	48
PUBLIC SERVICE BROADCASTING INTERVIEW	49
THE CAMARADERIE OF SODIUM LIGHTS	50
IN PRAISE OF URBAN LIVING	51
THE DRUNKENESS OF THINGS BEING VARIOUS	52
STARS AT THE BACK OF THE HOUSE	53
ART HISTORY OF EMIGRATION	54
NEXT TO, OF COURSE, GOD, IRELAND	55
TICKETS TO REMOTE AREAS OF PURE SILENCE	56
THE FUNDAMENTAL FACT OF MODERN IRISH HISTORY	57
IRISH	58
THE STREETS LIGHTING OUT OF ME	59
ON THE CORE OF NATIONAL IDENTITY BEING FOUND AT PERIPHERAL LOCATIONS	60
AIRPORT	61
THE BEAUTIFUL LONG FACTORIES OF ELECTRIC NIGHT	62
PROFILE	63
ASYLUM SEEKER'S ACCOMMODATION MANUAL	64
THE FORGOTTEN SPACE	65
IRISH ABROAD ELDERLY ADVICE NETWORK	66
THE MAN MADE OUT OF SHIPPING CONTAINERS	67
DENOTING THOSE PARTS OF THE FORM THAT MUST BE COMPLETED	68
ABOUT THE AUTHOR	70

I LOVE A MAN

for Sean Gallagher

I love a man who drinks whiskey for breakfast
and you have to be a gifted kind
to love a man who drinks whiskey for breakfast
and write a poem
for a man who drinks whiskey for breakfast
or imagine flowers and a midnight dance
with a man who drinks whiskey for breakfast
who has so much of the cosmos inside him
that he drinks whiskey for breakfast
whose love is the love of a bear in the high forest
drinking whiskey for breakfast
who travels the snowline in a vest and pants
drinking whiskey for breakfast
who lies but is not dishonest is true
and drinks whiskey for breakfast
who would gather the lost to him in laughter
as he drinks whiskey for breakfast
making them all feel gifted enough
to love a man who drinks whiskey for breakfast.

THE BEST DAY EVER, ASRAEL

after Brian Whelan

That was the best day ever,
> when you came back early and took me upstairs.

The best day ever,
> down by the canal and buses in clouds.

The best day ever,
> jiving and the bare bulb.

The best day ever,
> with a lost key and the taxi leaving.

The best day ever,
> waiting in the street for you to come down.

The best day ever,
> barely moving and sunshine leaking through the room.

The best day ever,
> when you leant your hand against my knee.

The best day ever,
> when you, with tinsel wings, came home with me.

THE GLISTENING SUN ON THE GLISTENING STREET

We live in the age of the city. The city is everything to us, it consumes us and for that reason we glorify it.

Onookome Okome

You are liquid in my arms
and the noises you make,
the way you utter,
because you are something
from the rain,
teeming beneath and above,

while doing this here,
when this place
already soaks us,
with an urgency
that can't
be contained,
the city ricocheting through us,

in the middle of day
rain in the window
from a place so far away,
fills me and fills you and fills me,
comes with you and comes with me and comes with you,
as if every address I ever had,

every snow dropped street,
every morning-shift kitchen,
every drunk living room,
was coming along too,
beside me and with me,

and I am falling from the house,
falling through an open window,
falling through the mirrored rain,
the pavement coming too,
the city glistening in the wet
and in the rain you waiting
there to catch me.

CONCEALMENT

In the city too
watching things themselves
is to repair our broken knowledge.

At the bus stop a kestrel
scatters sparrows
and there is sky above traffic.

To this place of reluctance
departing birds come.
A fox steals from a bin.

There is a shore of broken glass
beneath swings.
We live
in the space between buildings.

LIFE ON PUBLIC TRANSPORT

to my sisters

Every low flying thing remembers us.
A backyard childhood
of unlined faces,
before we build, assiduously,
our sadness.
Bees and everlasting dragonflies,
stolen trees and unseen creatures,
a football pitch, built and marked
in the shadow of the shadow
of failing industries.
Lines and lines of red, pigeon filled palaces.

We can't bring it back,
even though,
it is still there.
Once we put our hands on it
it changes shape, drifts, becomes smoke.
Winter was best,
watching television from the floor,
forked bread against the element.
Upstairs the landing light,
left on forever,
in case we got lost.

CHANGE OF ADDRESS

Bomb peck was our casual reference
for all the brick holed wastelands
still potted through the city
when the Irishman took us,
hand in hand,
three to each side,
to where our council rehousing stood
and the Irishwoman,
looking out on a sea of knee high green,
had swept an empty, silent room.

WORKING NIGHTS WHILE THE POETS READ

Poetry: I give you leave of absence

Sukanta Bhattacharya

In another world poets read
and they whisper
sweet profanities to the planets,
while the clock
goes on imagining
the instant of the clock
going off imagining
and the poets fool
the midnight birds to song,
cup madness in their palms,
while the wish for life to vanish
and time limping forward, stops,
time limping forward, stops,
and alphabets, stutter, dance
alphabets, stutter, dance
and this show
of glorious, utter, uselessness
as the dawn fully rises,
as the poets read,
while the air
shivers.

THE MAPS YOU TOOK WITH YOU
WHEN YOU WENT

the link between me and the factories
is broken, I have no money

Margaret Atwood

When we tatted around the back
there was a kid in a derelict toilet
sniffing glue as if this was
some film of urban deprivation.
You smoked in the open air unconcerned.
The last free man.

At home the light beneath our Sacred Heart
never ceased its red insistence
and those lost accents continued
their meandering accumulation.
Alcoholism, cancer and accident waited.

And I'm going back there now,
to walk the red brick length,
the disused road to Mass,
the cold, forgotten Angels,
and as I'm passing
I'll do what you did,
take off this shirt and fight
myself bare chested in the street.

IMPERIAL ROAD

Drinking on the doorstep with men in suits,
morning wedding bells muffled,
the honey coloured cold tea whiskey
laying a black gravel
across the road of our throats,
and clink a glass
against the ferocious
continuance of the city,
and all that lies in wait
suspended by your laughs
and your unflinching refusals,
the wedding suits dancing up the road
and the calendar for ever marked.

UNLAWFUL OATHS

Your desire for silence is perfect.
The factory of unlawful oaths
and the hollow, juddering air
leaves you here, at clock's end,
straining for silence and a smile.
In the instance of stillness is your release.

On nights you are gone you sleep during daylight,
appear downstairs like the unexpected life you've found
is fragmenting;
surprised at the sight of your life
watching you pass.

I put my hand in yours
and you watch me
put the ball in the net,
in the back of the net,
in front of watching thousands
crammed in to our backyard,
the blood music
we hear from our kitchen.

When your dream against the odds
fades at the post
you chase the greying
with muttered denials
and a construction of your own unlawful oaths;
insisting as it falls
on your own silent ability,
through the tattered concordance,
to rise again.

WE WENT TO SCHOOL IN A BALLOON

This is what it was like by the railway tracks we loved
because they were the only geography we ever saw
until the day the hot air balloon beached
and each one of us watched through railings
at the imagined century to come
and Eddie Nealand, Miss, lives in a house like a cave
on Inkerman Street and isn't that something, Miss,
to do with one of the wars and the Holy Communion picture
of Belinda Shields, Miss, got thrown in the rainbow
by the oil and soot beneath the arches of the viaduct
carrying trains from this city to another.

AFTER THE BATTLE OF SALTLEY GATES

They made the shed
out of Cork and Roscommon,
from sleepers going to Crewe, Preston, Sheffield,
Newcastle on a moonlit day,
metal roof from Saltley Gates,
coke stains leached to the sky,
men in the company of men,
of their own redundant time,
of work and shifts and drinking,
the vanished class raising the roof,
raising a laugh,
to the memory of itself.

LOVE SONG

In the city
write things down in silence.
It is easy to find,
on a street, a bus, a train.
The mislaid home.
Write in the margin.
It will be seen there.
It will be remembered.

Write the city
when no one else is looking.
On the pristine roof,
surprised by corners, by chimneys.
On parchment and vellum.
Everything is fixed.
In silence the city
writes things down.

THE CITY IS FUNDAMENTAL

for John Hankard

The city is fundamental,
a promised response
to heels kicking on the corner
or a station from which
no trains ever leave,
a blank geography
where ancestry is not decoded
and who you came from
is merely where you came from,
says what it means to your face
and the necklace of distant lights
cares as little for you
as it possibly could
and your fevered concerns
are only the city's own.

LATE NIGHT NOTES OF THE EMIGRANT

The little place with its little obsessions
and its endless anthologising of itself;
the mountain pony's coat and Ballyrush
making the whole world a local row,
until there's nothing left to ache,
nothing left unsaid
in a place those left
refuse to accept
is like the past
and is best understood
at a distance.

THE ECONOMIC SYSTEM
IN A TIME OF SURPLUS

With this
high rise living
they have given
the illusion of escape
and on account
of socio-economic strictures
inform us illusion
is the finest,
the most bounteous,
gift we could
have ever had.

A WHOLE SENSIBILITY

*A certain number of years
lived without money are enough
to create a whole sensibility*

Albert Camus

Pity you then,
inured and withered
by plenty,
inoculated
beyond human understanding.

THE SOUND OF PUBLIC SPACES

The city is a state
of habitual confusion
and within its foreground sirens
the older brick lines
of disregarded addresses
crackle the rigged electricity
of favelas and the slum,
the long defeat of silence
echoed in the crumbling streets
of inner city splendour
and the promise
of a crystalline, untrodden, lucidity.

LOST AFTERNOONS
after Fred Voss

I wanted to be
with them on a Sunday after Mass,
getting drunk in Sunday best suits they'd arrived in,
a fenced life of women and children,
further than corporeal,
a chaser of distaste for themselves,
for leaving in the first place I wanted

to be under suspicion
because of my voice I wanted to get up,
half-cut on a Monday morning
and go into a job I loathed
looking for extra hours to justify
so many kids on so many streets
sounding like somebody else's son,

I wanted the safety net
of being from somewhere left,
low wage silence
composing
with little subtlety,
I wanted,
those lost afternoons to go on and on.

GREEN FIRST SPACES FORM THE CORE OF URBAN LIVING

Before everything
we sat in your car
in the woods
and rain rioted
across the roof.

The world had just
begun and some unseen bird,
flying out of a clearing,
said we did not
have to speak,
so you didn't clear
the windscreen and very soon
the rain was water
at our laps and we floated
by deserted paths,
breaking out the doors,
becoming jetsam,
until swimming
past the trees
we made it out to sea
and those who knew us
never heard from us again.

Before that
we sat in your car
in the woods
and rain rioted
across the roof.

LIKE CLOCKWORK

They think that I will come,
stealing wallets and mobile phones,
throwing chairs around the accident and emergency.
I have to say to them
that between here and there
there is a long list of leavings.
The city remembers, I tell them,
departures, goings, not-belongings,
is he working out of town?

And I am the one that left, I say,
standing at the microphone,
explaining
why I use
the words I do.

We raise our glasses of white wine.
Later on, in the accident and emergency,
I am as surprised as anyone
to find
the chair
raised
above my head.

ALL YOUR RELATIVES DISTANT AND CLOSE GATHER BY THE RIVER THAT RUNS THROUGH EACH CITY

Down by the river
every drink you ever took
makes its way through your face
and the channels of your cheeks
to the belligerent, caustic,
pleading of your eyes.
Your jack-in-the-box shuffle.
Every synapse burnt by every last shot,
every pin-point reassurance that flipped
like a rancid organ
or an oral cancer,
like the misused pet reneging
with spiralling fear and suspicion,
to lurk amongst the remains of your refusal,
your unending refusal,
and all the last stands,
of the long, wide river.

THE COUNTY COUNCILLOR'S HOUSE

We fell away behind the warehouse.
All those people in their gladrags
and you couldn't set flame to a bottle, I whispered,
I am jumping out of my skin
and in to yours.

You pissed in the engine.
But I put a spanner in the electronic gate, I pilfered
the deeds to an apartment in Bulgaria
for I am tired,
of the county councillor's house.

YOU BRING OUT THE CITY IN ME

after Sandra Cisneros

I came looking for a fox,
the urgent smell by an orchard
and the flightless duck snatched
beneath the old forest splash
of a crab apple.
But you bring out the city in me,
the rich, stinking vinegar and the talk
like knives flashing or shots
amongst a night time map of lights.

You bring out the shopping trolley in the canal in me.
You bring out the moody, good-looking swagger in me.
You bring out the political marches and the belly fire in me.
You bring out the swearing made art and sprayed like graffiti in me.
You do, yeh you do, you fucking do.

You bring out the book in me.
The one called Death of a Football Hooligan. In me.
You bring out the terraces in me.
The swaying crush of identities tied to forgotten streets and factories in me.
The eruptions of life like psychosis in me.
The switchback blade of words in me.
You bring out all the prizes in me.
The nuclear explosion dream in me.

You bring out dark streets in me.
The waiting on the doorstep for a nightshift dad in me, for a late taxi
or a lost love in me.
You bring out the slot machine thrown to the floor in me, the huddle
outside the chip shop in me.
You bring out the afternoon drinking in me,
the knowing this will go too far in me.
You bring out the tiled corridors of worker's pubs in me,
the flimsy camaraderie in me.

You bring out the great escape ending of this Steve McQueen movie in me,
the city in me.
Yeh, I think you, you bring out the me in me.

I came looking for a fox,
the deep coloured wild beneath trees
and the wind pushing through old paths,
like everything mislaid remembered.
But, you, instead.
You bring out the city in me.

BIRMINGHAM

When we had finished,
in that cleft of rocks by a dirtied sea,
you said, that if there was an ocean,
my running down your legs
and your running down my legs
would leak into it
and be swallowed by gulls
whose droppings would feed the plankton
that would feed the whales
that would swim
away to Antarctica
and mate in the ice
with us inside them
until their running
evaporated into clouds
and came back to us in rain
that would come back up our taps,
so I rushed home,
with black oil on my trousers,
and drank cold tap water all night long,
drank you
for as long as I could,
sitting in the silence
of streaming cars below,
packs of them
drifting by on the ring road,
so that I could be in the Antarctic with you
and we would always be in the blue ice,
making noises
no one understood.

MODES OF TRANSPORT AS A SPIRIT LEVEL SIGNIFIER OF CLASS STRUCTURE

You are asked by one who knows better,
it being an international holiday,
a time of selling and drinking and comparing,
when no body is toiling or clocking on, nobody,
what brings you to work tomorrow,
as if you might be party to some explosive concept
or committed to some global, screen spread deadline
and when you miscomprehend and lower your drink
to say, ah, I'll get a lift, I hope, a taxi if I'm stuck,
because, as you know, no trains or buses,
he takes the gentle time to explain his mere
bewilderment that anyone works on days like these,
not, he begs forgiveness, his interest in modes of transport
and your staring at canyons and fault lines and rift valleys
is a long, long look at something very far away.

THREE O'CLOCK FIXTURE LIST

The city will follow you
Constantine Cavafy

Let's go to the old game.
There are people coming out of doors
with colours on
and the blue, blue sky.

Let's create our identities.
From the workshop and the factory and the yard
there are songs welling up,
swearing and cigarettes in the wind

and the blue, white, blue
and the blue, blue sky.

Let's surge to the pulsing thousands.
This invisible well
in the common fields
and the shout, clap, shout.

Let's merge in spontaneous illegality.
This, the closest thing
with malice and belonging
and the self-defining melee

and the blue, white, blue
and the blue, blue sky.

We were raised on the terraces.

WHAT HAPPENED AFTERWARDS

for Paul Gething

On the way to Mass
he was smashing up their house.
'You fucker! You fuck!'
Opposite them a wall
the length of the whole street;
work being done in industrial nations,
hearts broken on the shift.

'Come away,' you said. 'Come away
from all of that.
There are flats above shops and books.
For most of the night I wear nothing
but the cover of you.'

'And finish it like this,' you said.
'Like this. Just bring scissors.
It's only fifteen floors up,
all the kids below are in love with me

and the stuttering motorbike is stolen.
Believe me, when those lines of vests,
those dresses, tracksuits, and sweet, sweet knickers,
fall from heaven,
our confetti love,
our passing gift to the sky,
we will watch from the balcony,
see multi-coloured rain
wash mushroom clouds away,
and leave forever on the bus
and never, ever get off.'

NIGHTSHIFT

A missing paycheque away
from financial chaos,
even those of us who don't,
smoke dream of fag breaks,

do things for money
in our Soviet posters
of the nobility of labour,
some savour two o'clock

when the restless soul is furthest out,
others three for being nearer,
some four if the summer sun
is rising in the east,

one of us swearing these hours
are spiritual retreats,
the rest of us looking at him,
look at time being made,

drift out of gates and half-lit
streets of the stolen world,
fold in to bed like ghosts,
let the made-up world begin.

THE REVOLUTIONARIES FIRST TAKE OVER THE STATE BROADCASTER

I don't have a radio show, Frank, so I can't
simply play the tracks I like without a care for the listener
or dedicate a whole show to her,
so what I did instead
was put on a nightly broadcast and hope she listened,
starting with Fred Voss and considering for a moment,
live on air, Grace, red light blunt on the wall,
the streets below in uproar,
the presidential guard in retreat,
making Voss the whole programme but then
I put on Geoffrey Lehmann's Spring Forest,
the early tracks, Lilian,
the solitary tear in the starry night,
Michael Hartnett's visceral, gentle, catechism,
Roy Fisher making jazz out of an industrial hole,
Geoffrey Charlton coming home from a nightshift,
the anonymous Irish blackbirds scribbled in a margin
and I can hear the explosions in the distance, Frank,
the sirens and the cacophony
of the last helicopter leaving
and I'm on a roll with Auden, of course, Refugee Blues maybe,
Brendan Cleary's Odes to Lager and Tony Harrison
with the skinhead by the grave,
Keats and Yeats, Grace, yeh, they were on my side
and I even snuck in Sillitoe, Kelman
and Anthony Cartwright though strictly speaking,
but what the hell, this isn't their frequency anymore, Lilian,
this is mine
and I just stick to the work,
this is my show and no one plays any jingles,
I'm the one here in the confessional, the studio,
this holy place and these holy fools,
this tumult, this ragged roar,
I'll spin what I like and she'll hear,
she'll listen, Frank, don't worry, kid,
I know she will.

ALL THE ADDRESSES IN ALL OF THE CITIES

I want to breathe in the pollution, stand in the rush hour queues
I want to freak out on the fumes, crush in the rush hour queues
Hylda Sims

Through the alleyway the moon
and local accents smoke the last one.
Summer dies in a red glow.

Inside the house parents from other places
and a dog scratching at the door.
All the young men are in love.

There's an owl at the top of Hobmoor Road
in the grounds of the psychiatric hostel.
The moon is a cataract and the lost fathers howl.

In the slits of a school tower
the dream of a thousand abandoned swifts.
Hope is in the sky.

The evening road is a river of lights
and there's an orchestra of discordance.
A million human minds conspire.

Through the alleyway a staunch kindness
and light after light extinguished.
In the shuttered sky
something of the moon persisting.

SONGS WE SING ABOUT OURSELVES

for Antony Owen

This jemmy,
here,
my gift to you,
our shirts
snagging on broken glass,
we live in an old factory,
you and I,
somewhere our fathers
plotted golden numbers,
somewhere else
always swirling
around their heads,
some other country sighing,
a caravan by the sea,
we make things with our hands
while someone else makes money,
gets paid,
the world
too much with us,
we climb,
you and I,
in to closed down places,
tell ourselves,
this is the act
of love,
an act of vast generosity
in the face of cold mathematics,
light a candle and agree
there is nothing
we couldn't do,
here,
this jemmy,
my gift
to you.

HIGHWIRE

You were the greatest trapeze artist
I've ever known,
meaning everything you ever did
just about came off
and though there's lots I don't remember
that doesn't matter
because what does,
between thousand-storey buildings,
suspended near comets,
no visible means of support
but a thin line and a pole,
is knowing,
falling is impossible.

We lived in the sky,
in the luxury
of planets of time wasted,
of bedsit billionaires,
to the trembling point now,
the ache in the calves,
that when you enter a room
half my life hasn't happened,
and there is the straight line knowledge
that given half a chance,
the same exuberant step
in to nothingness again.

THOUGH WHEN THEY CATCH MY EYE
for Bernadette Edmead

I like the desperate for fags people.
I like that we're all on this bus together
and that no one minds I'm writing a poem.
I even like the one who's threatening to find
a fictional gangster from a television show
and get someone fucking sorted out.
I admit,
I even,
like her.

I like the philosopher who sits at the front
and says you've got to have a laugh, driver,
at the end of every sentence she utters
and I believe she has empirically
tested that proposition
and found it, to be true.
I like her,
maybe,
best of all.

I like the beautiful boy who's going in to town
on that first date,
sweeping his phone and sweatshop finery
as if getting updates
from the stock market of his inner life,
toying in his mind and hands
with changing his status.
We all
love him
a little bit.

I like that the desperate for fags people and the philosopher
and the driver and the beautiful boy and the poet
are showing the true existence of society
and that we are all genuinely in this together,
whilst hiring hit men, laughing and maybe,
I don't know, having sex, are all possible
on a public transport that is, after all,
the acme of social living in one place or another.

I like
all of this
very much.

WAITING TO BEGIN WHAT WORK IS

On shiftwork the chair
is a person in the night
wearing yesterday's clothes,
wearing the fidgeting
and light laden city,
the street shaped, scuffed accent,
the men sacked for striking,
for turning up weary from drink
and the rain
is an agreement, a settlement
for all the people wearing nothing,
wearing themselves,
until the lightening
on the bedside,
the birth pangs
of a far off universe,
the numbers of a place
that doesn't yet exist.

PUBLIC SERVICE BROADCASTING INTERVIEW

I don't have an exact date
for when I last went home
and, to be honest, I have a habit
of saying home here too, in this place.
I don't mean it.
I don't mean it about either of them.
I might as well say anywhere
beneath the moon.
But you can't say that kind of thing
where I come from.
Might as well say in my Sunday best
in the middle of the Irish Sea.
None of it is true. Not all of it.

I haven't walked those streets in so long, you see,
and caught an unexpected night
ferry to arrive.
Might as well say that.
Even that's not true though.
Truth is, I'm keeping home just here,
just there, just around the corner, just out of sight.
I'll turn and find it. I will.
I don't have an exact date,
so until then,
this will have to do.
There. I've said it now.

THE CAMARADERIE OF SODIUM LIGHTS

When the street is cathedral silent
I am in the bedroom working sleep
from a night inside the warehouse,
blinking in the cave trace
of all their working nights,
the camaraderie
of sodium lights,
the fog lost blackbird
singing to the dark,
all my vanished fathers'
invisible hours,
as if I lie
in someone else's form,
inhabit a shared, shaded state,
of filings, asbestos and paint,
the stratum we leave behind
brought out to sunlight for others
to pencil separate
and reconstruct some fabulous dream
of how they think
we lived.

IN PRAISE OF URBAN LIVING

My mother lived
in a Dutch painting
and it contained
her entirety,
an immigrant woman
she believed
in all manner of things
and knew others
with a certainty
that belied
her underlying anxiety,
so when she said,
if you make people live
in a pig sty
what will they
live like,
will they fill
baby's bottle with cola,
or God save us
from the self-made man,
I wouldn't let
a man make me,
I wouldn't let him near me
in a blue fit,
she was really saying,
where I come from
the sky is shattered with stars,
she was really saying,
she was muttering,
you are
my unceasing prayer,
do not worry,
here,
join my hand.

THE DRUNKENESS OF THINGS BEING VARIOUS

She likes the sound of her own voice,
likes the way it doesn't quite fit
the shape of wherever she is,
not true enough to the place she left,
the buddleia sprouting brick
and the silent chimneys
are all there,
the sound of the factory inside her mouth,
but not part of this place all the same,
whatever about the certain
intonations and turns of phrase
she has picked up,
after all these years of sounding
like someone else
she likes
as the years ahead
drop towards silence
that she has all this history
on her lips.

STARS AT THE BACK OF THE HOUSE
for Jill and Dom

Too many years ago now, at the end of each shift
                       I would go to the back of the house
and attempt a clear mathematics of my life,
not the making-ends-meet sums
but the invisible figurations I'd heard
the universe contained,
              displayed,
I considered what might add up and might not,
        sitting in the city at the back of the house
trying to sum up clarity and clearness
with starfields or snow that I'd walked
across safe in seeing all of the landscape
as if in snow light night I'd make it back
              to camp.

Everyone sits out sometimes with a smoke or a drink
                like me in the house on the street
in the city making delicate deliberations and mind sums
asking why this time of day added up for me,
whether something about receding light and beyond sight
movement, flight of birds and clouds,
              people drifting in a caesura
and linger thinking mathematics more than language
              was most abused and mistreated
by figures men and salesmen and opinion men
and that shapes never push themselves forward
but must be sought by all those sitting out
catching an obtuse geometry and wondering
              how to get this thing to hang.

ART HISTORY OF EMIGRATION

It is strange
that we hang
in dark suits
and v-neck geansaí,
our ties and black shoes,
rows of us
along the wall
and in the foreground
our uneven townland
of space-black drinks,
our collars
and hardened hands
in framed perspective
always reaching out
across the copper dented tables,
the impression and colour
of wordless listening,
to an indifferent sea.

NEXT TO, OF COURSE, GOD, IRELAND

We can't all live on a small island
      Brian Lenihan

On a small island
the mathematics of emigration
is always the same sum;
the same people go
so that the same people stay.

TICKETS TO REMOTE AREAS OF PURE SILENCE

Silence
was where they went to.
They came over borders mute
at passport control,
in and out,
on and off,
trains and boats.

For the benefit,
the welfare of those
who continue,
they went
where they were supposed to.

We are erecting a plinth
to show our gratitude
for their leaving,
their unstinting,
silence.

THE FUNDAMENTAL FACT
OF MODERN IRISH HISTORY

Emigration, perhaps, the fundamental social fact of modern Irish history.
R. F. Foster

I have to go along with all the others,
the thousands and thousands,
away from the island too small
for us all to live on,
quietly resigned to my role.
     I have to pass with them,
from parents and brothers and sisters
to live in English cities and become
every day the place I left behind as every day
the place I left behind departs.
     I have to climb into stereotype
and work with my callused hands and build
a family with foreign accents and hold
their skin to me
beneath someone else's sky.
     I have to bless each day that I left
and am left to feel that cardiac tightness
slip upon me and remind me that home
is in the past and I am always
from somewhere else.
     I have to set fire to the decades,
blaze through the contented histories,
illuminate the Irish faces just to show,
the lived and left existence,
to light as bright as I can their passing.

IRISH

to my brother

Even when the boats had cleaved away
they gathered in strip lit halls
in road facing clubs with predictable names;
The Emerald, The Shamrock, John Mitchell's,

they came beneath ring roads and an expanse
of city lights strung out
in a mixture of exhaustion and vigour
each and every county

of the small island expanded,
surrounded by the sounds of somewhere else
and the vanished generation expounding loyalties
nobody back home remembers,

insisting above the tumult and downpour
of this stretched place
on being who they were
and were always meant to be.

THE STREETS LIGHTING OUT OF ME

I don't want to die for Ireland, England, Birmingham or Cork.
I don't want to die for any of those nations, cities, places, notions.
I don't want to die for any flag.
I don't want to die

but when I do, and I will, I've decided,
I'll die for something I don't yet know.
Not for belonging,
which is only saying to the other,
you don't,

not for nationalism,
which is only a form of civil war.
No, for something with those I love gathered by.
I'll die for something

on a headland,
looking awkwardly out to sea
and the waves of equidistance,
the city streets lighting out of me,
showing me the way home.

ON THE CORE OF NATIONAL IDENTITY BEING FOUND AT PERIPHERAL LOCATIONS

for David Morris

The dunes, if you look at them,
are just grittier waves and the waves
are the dunes in motion,
leaving or arriving
and it is the gaps,
the necessary spaces,
that make them waves and dunes,
that define them, if you look at them,
and that reflected
the seagull's wings in flight
are dunes in the sky
or waves beside a cloud,
so that, if you look at them,
there is only the one shape
and it is the gaps instead,
the spaces in between them,
immaterial margins,
that make the shape,
so that, if you look at it,
the disregarded bit, there,
the off-centre,
is the core.

AIRPORT

after the Report of the Mahon Tribunal

What you have heard is true.
So don't let them cry out
as we leave.
Don't spare them indignation and disgust
as we depart.
For the television news.
Don't even let them shake their heads.
They didn't shake their heads
when we were shaking ours.

And I will do them a deal.
Here on the concourse as we go;
if they will not speak of me,
will not put me on the news as if,
I was their concern.
Let us deal. Let us be done.
Then I'll be off. Shake. Here.
I have spat in my hand.

THE BEAUTIFUL LONG FACTORIES OF ELECTRIC NIGHT

Some fearful men are ashamed to go home
and their women's children
sound
like another country
and
identities grow
from the tops
of their heads
and
each one of them
is the finest artist
the other has ever met.

PROFILE

> *A person without a city, beyond human*
> *boundary, a horror, a pollution to be avoided.*
>   Sophocles

I'll be alright when they come,
the way I speak,
speaking like we've always lived
here I can pass.
I don't know what you're going to do.
How do you expect to get by
sounding like that,
with that look on your face,
of something other,
like a field or a bare hill,
in a place like this
so out of place something,
not quite right.

ASYLUM SEEKER'S ACCOMMODATION MANUAL

This could be a doctor's waiting room anywhere,
pregnant with suffocation and forms
filled in long, cramped halls,
the stagnant river of institutional lighting,
a place the devouring rich
and the citizens of heaven
send the citizens of earth.

THE FORGOTTEN SPACE

It is a portrait of no one there
Gordon Burn

Sometimes we think,
what is there
in the space where we used to be,
the forgotten space.

And sometimes we think,
running counter to this,
is there room
for the space where we should be.

And here, even here,
nowhere near the space where we should be,
we sometimes think,
on occasions,
once or twice,
that we see you
in the streets,
in the space where we should be.

IRISH ABROAD ELDERLY ADVICE NETWORK

My country is in my face
and I have left that place
for good.

My fields are inside this room
and I am glad that I will never
go home.

The fury of youth is ash
and I have worked for so long
at being absent.

When I am found in this chair
leave me this is where
I belong.

THE MAN MADE OUT OF SHIPPING CONTAINERS

I never knew
I would forever be landing,
would become
the transport I arrived on.

I am always here,
newly minted like counterfeit,
I don't know,
if I am coming or going.

And solace,
such a predictable penance,
I am weary
each time I open the door.

If my life were cut open
this is how time could be told,
by these rings
on the counter.

DENOTING THOSE PARTS OF THE FORM THAT MUST BE COMPLETED

If this was to be,
my last sodden testament,
my rubble note,
then I am citizen.
Of places that never used to be,
that have just come into being.
Of redefinition
and reaffirmation.
Of small streams
of reiteration and marginal
fields.
Of false starts and blind alleys.
Of ill-drawn boundaries
where the inarticulate,
waiting in camps,
get their chance
to inhale
all the beautiful air
of the world.
There.

JOSEPH HORGAN was born in Birmingham, England, of Irish immigrant parents. He has lived back in County Cork since 1999. He is a poet, author, journalist, and reviewer. The author of seven previous books, amongst his credits are The Patrick Kavanagh Award, twice being awarded an Arts Council Bursary, his second book being serialised on RTE Radio One, and his fourth book being a Poetry Society Recommended Read. He has also been shortlisted for The Hennessy Award and nominated for The Ted Hughes Award. His work has been anthologised and published throughout Ireland, Europe, and the USA. He writes a popular column for *The Irish Post*.

Author Photo: Rangzeb Hussain

salmonpoetry

Cliffs of Moher, County Clare, Ireland

"Publishing the finest Irish and international literature."
Michael D. Higgins, President of Ireland